The Alamo

Ted and Lola Schaefer

Heinemann Library
Chicago, Illinois

© 2006 Heinemann Library
a division of Reed Elsevier Inc.
Chicago, Illinois

Customer Service 888-454-2279

Visit our website at www.heinemannlibrary.com

Designed by Richard Parker and Mike Hogg Design
Illustrations by Jeff Edwards
Originated by Chroma Graphics (Overseas) Pte.Ltd.
Printed and bound in China by South China Printing Company

10 09 08 07 06
10 9 8 7 6 5 4 3 2 1

Library of Congress Cataloging-in-Publication Data
Schaefer, Ted, 1948-
  The Alamo / Ted and Lola M. Schaefer.
    p. cm. -- (Symbols of freedom)
  Includes bibliographical references and index.
  ISBN 1-4034-6662-9 (library binding-hardcover) -- ISBN 1-4034-6671-8 (pbk.)
1. Alamo (San Antonio, Tex.)--Juvenile literature. 2. Alamo (San Antonio, Tex.)--Siege, 1836--Juvenile literature.
3. Texas--History--To 1846--Juvenile literature. 4. San Antonio (Tex.)--Buildings, structures, etc.--Juvenile
literature. I. Schaefer, Lola M., 1950- II. Title. III. Series.
  F390.S33 2005
  976.4'03--dc22
                                2005002010

Acknowledgments
The publishers would like to thank the following for permission to reproduce photographs:
Art Archive/ National History Museum Mexico City/ Dagli Orti p. 10; Bridgeman Art Library pp. 19, 17 (Private Collection, Roger-Viollet, Paris); Corbis pp. 4, 21, pp. 14 (D. Boone), 16, 20, 29 (Bettman), 23 (Hal Lott), 27 (Lowell Georgia), 13 (Sandy Felsentha); Getty Images pp. 11, 18 (Hulton Archive); Mary Evans Picture Library p. 5; Peter Newark's Americana Pictures pp. 7, 8, 9, 15, 22, 24; Picture Desk/ Kobal p. 12; Popperfoto pp. 25, 28.

Cover photograph of the Alamo reproduced with permission of Corbis (Randy Faris).

Some words are shown in bold, **like this**. You can find out what they mean by looking in the glossary.

Contents

The Alamo

The Alamo is a famous **shrine** in San
Antonio, Texas. In 1718 the Spanish built
a **mission** there. They taught Native
Americans about **religion** and farming.

Much later, Texans used the Alamo as a
fort. In 1836 they fought for their **freedom**
from Mexico. This was called the Battle of
the Alamo.

Settlers Move West

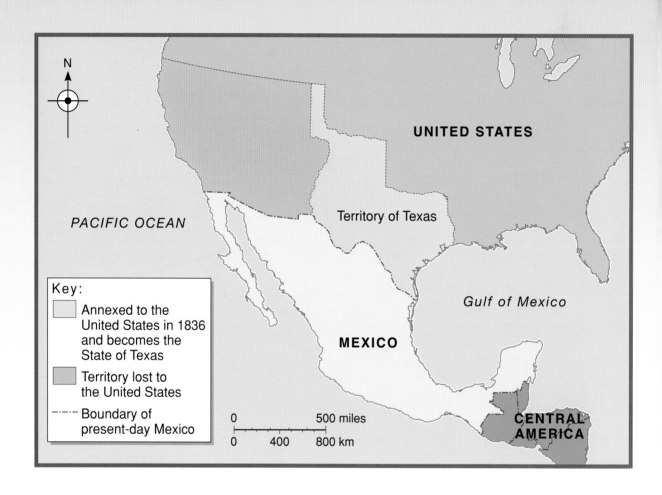

In the early 1800s, Mexico owned land called the Territory of Texas. Very few people lived there. **Settlers** were welcome to come and buy land.

Settlers could buy more than 4,000 **acres** of land for $30. They could grow crops and keep cattle. People from all over the country moved to Texas.

Divided Texans

Stephen Austin led many **settlers** into Texas. At first they were happy to live under Mexican rule. These settlers were called the "Peace Party."

Other settlers became unhappy living under Mexican rule. These people wanted **independence**. They formed the "War Party," led by Sam Houston.

General Santa Anna

General Santa Anna became **president** of Mexico in 1831. He was angry with the **settlers** in Texas who wanted **independence**.

General Santa Anna wanted to drive the settlers out of Texas. He planned a surprise **attack**. The Mexican Army marched north through winter storms.

Before the Battle

General Santa Anna led the Mexican Army into southern Texas. He had thousands of soldiers marching and riding horses. They brought guns and cannons.

The Texans saw the Mexican Army coming. They all came to the Alamo. They packed the walls and doors with dirt and logs. Their **fort** was ready for battle.

Leaders of the Alamo

William Travis led the men at the Alamo. He was a lawyer trained as a soldier. He had not been in many battles.

James Bowie was a **trapper** and a land salesman. David Crockett, shown here, was a hunter and Congressman from Tennessee. They both led **volunteers** to the Alamo.

Trapped in the Fort

On February 23, 1836, Mexican soldiers
surrounded the Alamo. For thirteen days
they dug **trenches** and moved closer. They
also fired cannons at the fort.

William Travis had less than 200 Texan fighters to **defend** the Alamo. He needed more men. He sent riders with letters asking for **volunteers** to come and help.

The Attack Begins

Early on March 6, 1836, the Mexican Army **attacked** the Alamo. More than 1,500 Mexican soldiers ran toward the **fort** in long lines.

Mexican soldiers attacked all four sides of the fort at the same time. The fighting was fast and hard. The Texans killed and **injured** many of Santa Anna's men.

The Last Fight

Hundreds of Mexican soldiers climbed over the walls of the Alamo. The Texan **settlers** fought bravely. But there were too many soldiers to fight!

The Mexican soldiers took control of the battle. After 90 minutes the fight was over. Almost all of the Texans were dead. The Mexican Army won the Battle of the Alamo.

Remember the Alamo

After the Battle of the Alamo, many Texan **settlers** were angry. Six weeks later Sam Houston and his men **attacked** the Mexican Army. They shouted, "Remember the Alamo!"

The Mexican Army was **defeated**. For ten years the Republic of Texas was **independent**. On February 19, 1846, Texas became part of the United States.

The Alamo Becomes a Shrine

After the Mexican Army went back to Mexico, the United States Army used the Alamo as a **storehouse**. Later the State of Texas used it as a general store.

Since 1905 the Alamo has been a **shrine**. It reminds us of the men who died fighting for **freedom**.

Visiting the Alamo

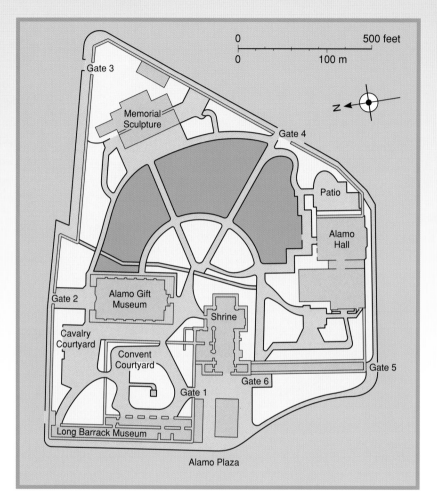

Two buildings of the old Alamo **fort** are still there. These are the **Shrine** and Long Barrack. In the Shrine, you can see David Crockett's vest, or a ring worn by William Travis.

These items remind us of these brave men. There is also a **memorial sculpture** at the Alamo. It shows some of the men who fought there.

Fact File

The Alamo

★ "Alamo" is a Spanish word meaning "cottonwood." Cottonwood trees were common in this area at the time.

★ To protect the Alamo from gunfire, Texans padded the walls of the **fort** with dirt. The walls had to be as thick as the length of a car to stop a cannonball.

★ William Travis fired a cannon three times a day – in the morning, at noon, and again at night. This sent a signal to **settlers** that the Alamo had not been taken by the Mexicans.

★ During the 13-day **attack** on the Alamo, Mexicans fired more than 300 solid cannonballs at the walls of the fort.

★ In 1960 a film was made about the Alamo. John Wayne played Davy Crockett. The photo on page 12 is from this film.

Timeline

The Alamo

★ 1718   Spanish set up the **Mission** San Antonio de Valero

★ 1744   Building of Long Barrack is finished

★ 1762   Work stopped on the mission church

★ 1833   Santa Anna becomes **president** of Mexico

★ 1836   Thirteen day battle of the Alamo by Santa Anna and the Mexican Army

★ 1836   Sam Houston **defeats** the Mexican Army at San Jacinto. Texas becomes **independent**.

★ 1846   Texas becomes the 28th state

★ 1883   State of Texas buys the church

★ 1903   Daughters of the Republic of Texas save the buildings of the Alamo and begin work to **restore** them

★ 1905   The Alamo becomes a **shrine**

Glossary

acre area of land almost the size of a football field

attack start fighting

defeat beat someone or win a battle

defend keep someone or something safe from harm

fort strong building, made to stand up to an attack

freedom having the right to say, behave, or move around as you please

independence not belonging to other people or another country

injure hurt or harm someone

memorial something that is built to help people remember a person or event

mission church or other building where missionaries live and work

president person chosen by the people of a country to be their leader

religion system of belief or worship

restore bring back to original condition

settler someone who moves to a new place and makes a home

sculpture something carved or shaped out of stone, wood, metal, marble, or clay

shrine place that is kept to remember important people or events

storehouse building used to keep supplies

surround to be on every side of something

trapper someone who makes a living by trapping wild animals, usually for their fur

trench long, thin ditch used to protect soldiers in battle

volunteer person who offers to help without being paid

More Books to Read

An older reader can help you with these books:

Britton, Tamara L. *The Alamo*. Edina, Minn.: ABDO, 2004.

Burgan, Michael. *The Alamo*. Minneapolis, Minn.:
  Compass Point, 2001.

Sipe, Antoinette Leonard. *The Alamo*. Philadelphia, Pa.:
  Mason Crest, 2004.

Sorensen, Lynda. *The Alamo*. Vero Beach, Fla.:
  Rourke, 1994.

Visiting the Alamo

The Alamo is open every day of the year except Christmas Eve (December 24) and Christmas Day (December 25). The opening hours are 9:00 A.M. to 5:30 P.M. Monday to Sunday, and 10:00 A.M. to 5:30 P.M. on Sunday. You do not have to pay to visit the Alamo. History talks are offered every 30 minutes, except during the lunch hour.

To ask for a brochure and map of the Alamo, write to this address:

The Alamo
P.O. Box 2599
San Antonio, TX 78299.

Index